tHe Country Friends® Collection

Crockery Cooking

Holly... can cook for a crowd with her big slow cooker.

Kate ...always forgets to plug it in.

Mary Elizabeth ...loves the convenience of Crockery Cooking.

How does this thing Work, anyway?

What a marvelous machine! A slow cooker operates continuously to cook your food while you're otherwise occupied. Most cookers hide their heating coils in their outer shell; when you turn the cooker on low, the coils heat up to around 200° and stay on to heat up your cooker's crockery lining. A high setting cranks the coil temperature up to about 300°.

Other slow cookers have a heating element in their base, and the heat cycles on and off to keep a constant temperature. Cool, huh?

A slow cooker is very energy-efficient since it operates on low wattage. (You can use the money you save on your electric bill to buy extra chocolate bars.)

Be sure to follow the manufacturer's instructions on taking good care of your crockery cooker. You want it to last a good, long time!

WHO CARES? Let's just eat.

...let it take care of supper.

★ SCRUMPTIOUS BBQ Sandwiches

a recipe from Francie Stutzman ★ Dalton, OH

3·LB. POT ROAST
¼ c. WATER
¼ c. MILK
2 T. VINEGAR
3 T. WORCESTERSHIRE SAUCE
1 t. CHILI POWDER
3 c. BARBECUE SAUCE
12 HAMBURGER BUNS

PLACE ROAST IN 4·QUART SLOW COOKER. ADD WATER, MILK, VINEGAR, WORCESTERSHIRE SAUCE & CHILI POWDER. COVER & COOK ON LOW FOR 10 TO 12 HOURS. 2 HOURS BEFORE SERVING, REMOVE ROAST & LIQUID FROM SLOW COOKER. SHRED MEAT & RETURN TO COOKER WITH BARBECUE SAUCE; COOK FOR ADDITIONAL 2 HOURS.

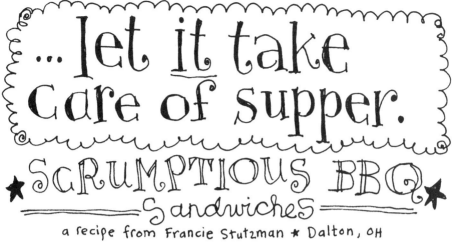

MAKES 12 SANDWICHES FOR YOUR COUNTRY FRIENDS!

5

I never eat when I can dine. ～ MAURICE CHEVALIER

Life * of * the * PARTY Snack Mix

a recipe from
Scott Harrington ★ Boston, MA

2 c. bite-size crispy wheat cereal squares

2 c. bite-size crispy corn cereal squares

2 c. bite-size crispy rice cereal squares

3 c. thin pretzel sticks

13-oz. jar mixed nuts

1 t. garlic salt

½ t. seasoned salt

2 T. grated Parmesan cheese

⅓ c. butter, melted

⅓ c. Worcestershire sauce

SEND A SLOW COOKER TO YOUR FAVORITE COLLEGE STUDENT WITH THIS RECIPE (and SAMPLES!) INSIDE!

In a large paper bag, mix together cereals, pretzels & nuts along with garlic salt, seasoned salt & cheese. Empty bag into a large bowl and place butter & Worcestershire sauce over mixture; combine gently with your hands. Empty bowl into a 4-quart slow cooker and cook on low for 3 to 4 hours. Tear open the bag used to originally mix the snack mix and spread flat on a counter. Spread heated snack mix onto bag and let dry for a minimum of 1 hour, letting the paper absorb excess moisture. Store in airtight containers. Makes about 10 cups.

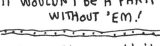

HOLLY'S
Teeny Weenies

IT WOULDN'T BE A PARTY
WITHOUT 'EM!

2 16-oz. Pkgs. cocktail weiners

12-oz. bottle chili sauce

12-oz. jar grape jelly

Combine all ingredients in a 3.½ quart slow cooker and cook on low for 6 to 8 hours. Makes 24 servings.

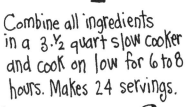

Good things come in teeny packages.

HOT CRAB DIP

a recipe from
JoAnn
★ Gooseberry Patch

3 8-oz. pkgs. cream cheese, cubed & softened
¼ to ½ c. milk
2 6.½ oz. cans crabmeat, drained
½ c. green onions, chopped
1 t. prepared horseradish
1.½ t. Worcestershire sauce

Combine all ingredients in a lightly greased 3.½ quart slow cooker. Cover and cook on high for about 30 minutes or until cheese melts; stir occasionally. Cover and continue to cook on high 'til mixture is smooth and cheese is melted. Add more milk if necessary; turn to low for 3 to 4 hours. Just before serving, remove cover. Makes about one quart.

Vessels large may venture more, but little boats should keep near shore.
-BENJAMIN FRANKLIN

Bring on the chips!

OLÉ DIP

a recipe from
Debbie Hopson
★ Whitesboro, TX

¡MUY BUENO!

15-oz. can Ranch-style beans
10-oz. can diced tomatoes
         with chilies
1 lb. ground beef, browned
1-lb. pkg. pasteurized process
         cheese spread, cubed
½ pt. whipping cream
Garnish: tortilla chips

In a 2-quart slow cooker, combine beans, tomatoes, ground beef and cheese. Cook on high for about 30 minutes or until cheese is melted. Turn cooker to low until one-half hour prior to serving; add whipping cream. Serve with chips. Makes 12 to 15 servings.

★ No Peeking! Unless the recipe calls for stirring, try not to lift the lid as your food cooks ~ it lets heat escape.

Sweet & Sour meatballs

a recipe from Mirti Murray ✱ Davie, FL

10.3/4 oz. can tomato soup
16 oz. can whole cranberries
1 T. grape jelly
1 t. lemon juice
1 lb. frozen meatballs, cooked

Mix soup & cranberries in a saucepan; bring to a boil. Add grape jelly & lemon juice. Remove from heat and pour over meatballs. Place all in a 6-quart slow cooker on low for 4 hours. Makes 20 to 30 servings.

Real friends always SHARE.

(even when they don't wanna.)

Good Honey • Garlic Chicken Wings

a recipe from
Mary Murray *
Gooseberry Patch

3 lbs. chicken wings, cleaned & halved
salt & pepper to taste
1 c. honey
½ c. soy sauce
2 T. oil
2 T. catsup
1 clove garlic, minced

Sprinkle chicken with salt & pepper. In a mixing bowl, combine remaining ingredients and mix well. Place chicken in a 4-quart slow cooker and pour sauce over. Cook on low for 6 to 8 hours. Makes 8 to 12 servings.

calico
BAKED BEANS

a recipe from Tracy Nordquist ★ South Coffeyville, OK

16·oz. pkg. bacon, crisply cooked & crumbled
2/3 c. barbecue sauce
1/3 c. catsup
3/4 c. brown sugar, packed
1 t. dry mustard
2 t. cider vinegar
16·oz. can pork & beans
16·oz. can butter beans, drained
15·oz. can kidney beans, drained

Mix all ingredients in a 4-quart slow cooker and simmer on low for 2 to 3 hours. Makes 8 to 10 servings.

"... and the calico cat replied,
"Mee-ow!"
— old childrens' poem —

Macaroni and cheese

a recipe from Stacie Seiders ★ OAKTON, VA

7·oz·pkg. macaroni, cooked
12·oz·can evaporated milk
3 eggs, beaten
1 stick butter, melted
Salt & pepper to taste
3 c. Cheddar cheese, grated & divided

Mix macaroni, milk, eggs
& butter. Add salt & pepper
and 2 cups cheese ;
stir well. Pour into a
5-quart slow cooker
and sprinkle with
remaining cheese.
Cover and cook on low
for 3 hours . Do not
take lid off until
ready to serve. Makes
12 servings.

I like a cook who
smiles out loud when
he tastes his
own work. - ROBERT F. CAPON

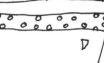

13

Aren't you glad your dinner's in the slow cooker?

SWISS STEAK
a recipe from Corrine Lane
★ Gooseberry Patch

1·½ lbs. round steak
2 T. all-purpose flour
1 t. salt
¼ t. pepper
1 c. celery, chopped
1 carrot, chopped
1 onion, sliced
15·oz. can tomato sauce

Cut steak into several serving pieces. Combine flour, salt & pepper ~ sprinkle over meat. Mix well and place in a 3-½ quart slow cooker. Add celery, carrot & onion. Pour tomato sauce over top. Cook on low for 8 to 10 hours. Makes 4 to 6 servings.

ARTICHOKE · CHICKEN PASTA

a recipe from Mary Luinstra * Great Falls, MT

16 oz. frozen grilled chicken breast strips
1 T. chicken bouillon granules
¼ c. water
17-oz. jar alfredo sauce
6-½-oz. jar marinated artichoke
        hearts, drained
6-oz. pkg. angel hair pasta, cooked
        (Makes 4 servings)

Place chicken strips in a 4-quart slow cooker with bouillon & water. Cook on low for 2 to 3 hours. One half hour prior to serving, turn cooker to high and place sauce & artichokes over chicken. Serve over pasta.

Ready and waiting!

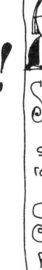

PSSST! SLOW COOKER SECRETS

from Mary Elizabeth

Some veggies take longer to cook in a slow cooker. Chop 'em up pretty good or slice 'em thin, especially with root veggies.

Save time on those oh-so-busy mornings by preparing your slow cooker ingredients the night before; chop vegetables, brown meat, set out other ingredients and just pop 'em in the pot in the a.m.!
(Of course, keep the prepared perishables in the fridge overnight.)

15

Super-simple to fix...

Farmhouse Dressing

a recipe from Karen Antonides ★ Gahanna, OH

1 c. margarine
1½ c. onion, chopped
2 c. celery, chopped
¼ c. parsley sprigs
2 8-oz. cans mushrooms, drained
12 to 13 c. dry bread cubes
1 t. poultry seasoning

1½ t. salt
1 t. sage
1 t. pepper
½ t. marjoram
3 to 4 c. chicken broth
2 eggs

Melt margarine in skillet, and sauté onion, celery, parsley & mushrooms. In a large bowl, pour mixture over bread cubes. Add seasonings and toss together. Pour in enough broth to moisten. Add eggs ~ mix well. Lightly pack into a 4-quart slow cooker.

Cover and cook on high for 45 minutes; reduce to low and cook for 4 to 8 hours.

Makes 12 to 14 servings.

16

... and **Down·Home Delicious!**

Scalloped Potatoes & Ham

a recipe from Pam Colden ★ Brodhead, WI

8 to 10 potatoes, sliced
2 c. ham, cubed
1 onion, diced
2 c. Cheddar cheese, shredded
10-3/4 oz. can cream of mushroom soup

Layer one ingredient at a time, starting with potatoes, ham, onion & cheese in a 5-quart slow cooker. When done layering, pour soup over all; do not mix. Cook on high for 5 hours, or on low for 8 to 10 hours.   Makes 6 to 8 servings.

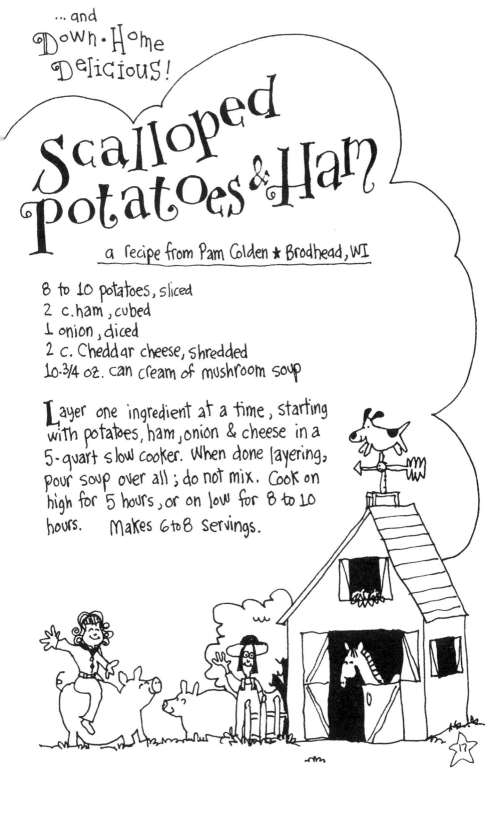

I can't believe you made this in a slow cooker. Broccoli Cheese Soup

a recipe from Sheila Bailey
* Watertown, WI

8 oz. pasteurized process cheese spread
2 10·3/4 oz. cans cream of celery soup
1 pt. half-and-half
2 10-oz. pkgs. frozen, chopped broccoli

Place all ingredients in a 3·½ quart slow cooker and cook on low for 6 to 8 hours. Makes 6 to 8 servings.

For easy clean-up, spray your slow cooker with a cooking spray before you begin.

☆ Broccoli (and other cruciferous veggies) is seriously good for you. They contain antioxidants and are high in fiber & vitamins. Eat up!

Chow·Down Corn Chowder

a recipe from Marian Buckley ★ Fontana, CA

6 slices bacon, diced
½ c. onion, chopped
2 c. potatoes, peeled & diced
2 10-oz. pkgs. frozen whole-kernel corn
16-oz. can cream-style corn
1·¼ T. sugar
1·½ t. Worcestershire sauce
1·¼ t. seasoned salt
½ t. pepper
1 c. water

In skillet, fry bacon until crisp. Remove bacon; reserve drippings. Add onion & potatoes to drippings and sauté for about 5 minutes; drain well. Combine all ingredients in a 3·½ quart slow cooker; stir well. Cover and cook on low for 4 to 7 hours. Makes 4 servings.

Chowder breathes reassurance. It steams consolation.
— CLEMENTINE PADDLEFORD —

19

Granny's Tater Soup

a recipe from Amy O'Connell
* New Ulm, MN

6 potatoes, peeled & chopped
2 leeks, chopped
2 carrots, chopped
1 stalk celery, chopped
4 cubes chicken bouillon
1 T. parsley flakes
5 c. water
1 T. salt
⅓ c. butter
chives, chopped to taste
12 oz. can evaporated milk

Place all ingredients, except chives & milk, in a 4-quart slow cooker. Cover and cook on low for 7 to 8 hours or on high for 3 to 4 hours. Stir in milk and chives during the last hour of cooking. Makes 8 to 10 servings.

Listen to your grandma. Eat it. It's good for you.

* JUST ADD HOT BREAD FOR A GOOD-TO-EAT MEAL!

20

A little of what you fancy does you good.

— MARIE LLOYD

a recipe from Kelly Elliott ★ Fairview, TN

1·½ lbs. ground beef, browned
1 onion, chopped
1 to 2 c. tomato juice
15·oz. can tomato sauce
2 10¾ oz. cans cream of potato soup
10·½ oz. can beef broth
2 15-oz. cans kidney beans, drained
1·¼-oz. pkg. taco seasoning mix
Garnish: corn chips, Monterey Jack cheese, shredded
           and sour cream

Combine all ingredients in a 5-quart slow cooker, heat on low for approximately 6 hours. Serve over corn chips and sprinkle on cheese and sour cream. Makes 6 to 8 servings.

Veggies in the Pot

Baked Potatoes

a recipe from Laura Fuller
* Fort Wayne, IN

12 potatoes,
  unpeeled & well greased

Fill a 4.½ quart slow cooker with potatoes. Cover and cook on low for 8 to 10 hours. No water is necessary!

Baked Sweet Potatoes

a recipe from Virginia Watson * Scranton, PA

6 sweet potatoes,
  unpeeled
¼ c. water

Place potatoes in a 4.½ quart slow cooker. Add water, cover and cook for 1 hour on high, then turn to low for 6 to 8 hours or 'til sweet potatoes are tender.

Fresh Green Beans

a recipe from Elizabeth Blackstone * Racine, WI

2 lbs. fresh green beans, chopped
3 to 4 c. water
1 t. salt
¼ lb. ham, cubed

Place all ingredients in a 4.½ quart slow cooker. Cover & cook on low for 10 to 12 hours. Stir occasionally. Makes 3 servings.

See? I can too cook something!

slow cooker Ham·sams a la Kate

1·½ lbs. cooked ham, finely chopped
1 c. brown sugar, packed
½ c. Dijon mustard
¼ c. green pepper, diced
1 T. instant minced onion
1 20·oz. can crushed pineapple, undrained

12 buns

Mix all ingredients (except the buns, of course — don't be silly!) in a 5·quart slow cooker. Cook on low for 3 to 4 hours. Uncover and cook on high for 15 to 30 minutes until the sauce is thickened. Stir and serve on buns. Makes 12 servings.

You are invited

Have a slow-cooker party on a Saturday night! Invite each friend to bring a slow cooker full of something good to eat — and have a feast!

Turn the pot on low
and
go play in the snow!

While you're
having fun

Your supper gets
Done!

Pot Roast
and
Veggies

a recipe from Donna Dye ★ London, OH

2 to 4-lb. pot roast
salt & pepper to taste
4 T. all-purpose flour
¼ c. cold water
1 t. browning sauce
1 clove garlic, minced
2 onions, coarsely chopped
5 potatoes, peeled & coarsely chopped
3 carrots, coarsely chopped

Place roast in a 4-quart slow cooker; sprinkle with salt & pepper. Make a paste of flour & cold water; stir in browning sauce and spread over roast. Add garlic, onions, potatoes & carrots. Cover and cook on low for 8 to 10 hours. Makes 4 to 6 servings.

Beefy Pot Pie

a recipe from Tonya Sheppard ★ Galveston, TX

2·lb. round steak, cubed
2 c. plus 3 T. all-purpose flour, divided
2 t. salt, divided
⅛ t. pepper
2 carrots, peeled & sliced
3 potatoes, peeled & sliced

1 onion, thinly sliced
16·oz. can whole tomatoes, drained
3 t. baking powder
¼ c. shortening
3/4 c. milk

Place steak in a 3·½ quart slow cooker. Combine 3 tablespoons flour, 1 teaspoon salt & pepper; coat steak thoroughly. Add carrots, potatoes, onion & tomatoes; mix. Cover and cook on low for 7 to 10 hours. One hour before serving, remove steak & veggies and pour into a shallow 2·½ quart baking dish. Combine remaining flour, salt & baking powder. Cut in shortening until mixture resembles coarse cornmeal. Add milk ∽ stir well. Pat out on floured board; roll out to cover baking dish. Bake, covered, at 425 degrees for 20 to 25 minutes. Makes 4 servings.

25

☆ TIP : IF YOU USE FROZEN VEGGIES, BE SURE TO THAW OR RINSE THEM IN WARM WATER BEFORE YOU PUT 'EM IN YOUR SLOW COOKER. OTHERWISE, THEY'LL KEEP YOUR DISH FROM HEATING UP AS QUICKLY TO THE PROPER TEMPERATURE!

Hey!
Look! Just Look! I ate my porkchop and my peas... I cleaned my plate!

So What's For Dessert?

TRIPLE TREAT
a recipe from Mel Wolk
★ St. Peters, MO

18·¼ oz. pkg. chocolate cake mix
1 pt. sour cream
3·½ oz. pkg. instant chocolate pudding mix
6 oz. pkg. chocolate chips
3/4 c. oil
4 eggs
1 c. water

Spray a 5-quart slow cooker with non-stick cooking spray. Mix together all ingredients and place in slow cooker. Cook on low for 6 to 8 hours, trying not to open lid. Serve with ice cream.

HOW much can I put in the pot?

Your slow cooker should be filled one-half to three-quarters full to operate well. Food will be more tender and tastier. Use the correct size crockery cooker for best results.

DOES "TRIPLE TREAT" MEAN I GET 3 SERVINGS?

Crockery CHERRY Cobbler

a recipe from
Sharon Velenosi
★ Garden Grove, CA

2 21-oz. cans cherry pie filling
18-1/4 oz. pkg. yellow cake mix
1/4 c. butter, softened
1/2 c. chopped nuts

Pour pie filling into a 5-quart slow cooker; spread evenly. In a large bowl, combine dry cake mix with butter 'til mixture is crumbly; sprinkle over pie filling. Sprinkle with nuts. Turn slow cooker on low, cover and cook for 3 hours. Serve warm from the pot. Great with ice cream or whipped cream. Makes 6 to 8 servings.

The good things in Life are not to be had SINGLY; but come to us with a MIXTURE.
— anonymous —

Cinnamon-Raisin Baked APPLES

a recipe from Zoe Bennett
★ Columbia, SC

2 T. raisins
1/4 c. sugar
6 to 8 apples, cored
1-1/2 t. cinnamon
2 T. butter
1/2 c. water

Combine raisins & sugar; fill center of apples. Sprinkle with cinnamon ~ dot with butter. Place in a 4-quart slow cooker; add water. Cover and cook on low for 7 to 9 hours. Makes 6 to 8 servings.

The ripest peach is highest on the tree.
— JAMES WHITCOMB RILEY

The sweetest peach is in the ...

Cinnamon Peaches

a recipe from Rhonda Reeder
★ Ellicott City, MD

1/3 c. SUGAR
1/2 c. BROWN SUGAR, PACKED
3/4 c. BISCUIT BAKING MIX
2 EGGS
2 t. VANILLA EXTRACT
2 t. MARGARINE, MELTED
5-OZ. CAN EVAPORATED MILK
2 c. PEACHES, MASHED
3/4 t. CINNAMON

Spray a 4–QUART SLOW COOKER WITH NON-STICK COOKING SPRAY. COMBINE SUGARS & BISCUIT MIX ᵔ ADD EGGS & VANILLA. BLEND IN MARGARINE & MILK. ADD PEACHES & CINNAMON. POUR INTO A SLOW COOKER. COOK ON LOW FOR 6 TO 8 HOURS. MAKES 3 to 4 SERVINGS.

Take along a slow cooker dessert to a party or meeting — simply wrap the pot in a towel to insulate it. Serve within an hour or plug it in on a low setting.

Lemon · Poppy Seed Cake

a recipe from Janet Pastrick
★ Gooseberry Patch

14·oz. pkg. lemon·poppy seed
bread mix
1 egg
8 oz. sour cream
1·¼ c. water, divided
½ c. sugar
¼ c. lemon juice
1 T. butter

Mix together bread mix, egg, sour cream & ½ cup water until well moistened. Spread batter into lightly greased 3·½ quart slow cooker. Combine sugar, lemon juice, butter & remaining water in small saucepan ~ bring to boil. Pour boiling mixture over batter; cover and cook on high for 2 to 2·½ hours. Edges will be slightly browned. Turn heat off ~ leave in pot 30 minutes with cover ajar. When cool enough to handle, hold large plate over pot, then invert. Makes 6 to 8 servings.

To JUICE A LEMON, here's a little trick:

Poke a teeny hole in the SKIN of the fruit ~ microwave on high for 10 or 15 seconds. Wait a minute, then roll the lemon on the countertop and CUT and Squeeze.

I want nothing to do with natural foods. At my age, I need all the preservatives I can get.
– GEORGE BURNS –

29

KATE'S

voice of experience

5 Things One Can·But·SHouldn'T Do with a Slow CookeR:

Wash sneakers in it.

PoP pop-corn. It won't work.

Make stewed peanut butter and jelly sandwiches.

Use it as a dog shampoo-er. IT JUST makes him mad.

Slow cook Easter dinner starting in February. CONDEMNED

Everything happens to everybody sooner or later if there is time enough.

— GEORGE BERNARD SHAW —

SAFETY FIRST!

Use these common-sense tips when slow cooking with meats!

★ Ground meats should be browned & drained before using in a slow cooker recipe to help destroy any bacteria in the meats.

★ Be sure all meats are thoroughly cooked. Slow cooker recipes that use raw poultry or beef should cook a minimum of 3 hours.

★ Whole chickens and other poultry are not good candidates for slow cookers— the meat pieces are so large they may not cook all the way through.

★ Thaw meat items in the fridge or a microwave. Thawing at room temperature is an invitation for food spoilage and worse.

In the unlikely case of Leftovers:

Don't leave 'em sitting in the slow cooker at room temperature for more than 1 hour!

Reheat leftovers in the microwave or on the stove. Reheating in the slow cooker is unsafe since it takes too long for the food to reach a safe internal temperature.

When in doubt, throw it out; if it's green, it's bad cuisine!

Gather ye Rosebuds
while ye may,
Old Time is
still a-flying.... ROBERT HERRICK

Go on ~ enjoy the time
you've got ~
thanks to your slow cooker pot!